THE ILLUSTRATED
BIRD

Love and Happy Birthday
to Bobby
from George and Rosemary
June 1982

THE ILLUSTRATED
BIRD

Edited by Maggie Oster
Designed by Sonja Douglas

A Tree Communications Edition
Dolphin Books/Doubleday & Company, Inc.
Garden City, New York 1978

Copyright © 1978 by Tree Communications, Inc. All rights reserved. No part of this work may be reproduced or transmitted in any form by any means, electronic or mechanical, including photocopying and recording, or by any information storage or retrieval system without permission in writing from the publisher. Published in the United States by Doubleday/Dolphin, Garden City, New York.

Printed in U.S.A.

ISBN 0-385-14576-4

Library of Congress Catalog Card Number: 78-61182

Created and produced by
Tree Communications, Inc.
250 Park Avenue South
New York, New York 10003

The editors gratefully acknowledge the assistance of the following: Anna Teresa Callen, picture research; Jane Opper and Wendy Schrock Dreyzin, text; Jack Hope, introduction; Mary Clarke, text editing; and Ruth Michel, copy editing and proofreading.

We also wish to acknowledge the assistance of the following: SCALA/Editorial Photocolor Archives for photos on the front cover and pages 9, 10, 11, 22, 23, 26, 27, 33, 48, 51, 53, 63, 65, 67, 71, 73, 75; Editorial Photocolor Archives for photos on pages 17, 24, 25, 61; Joseph Martin/ Editorial Photocolor Archives for photos on pages 15, 39, 62, 69; Hubert Josse/Editorial Photocolor Archives for photos on pages 35, 79; Bruce Anspach/Editorial Photocolor Archives for the photo on page 60. The engravings on pages 1, 3, 4 are from *1800 Woodcuts by Thomas Bewick and His School,* Dover Publications, New York. The engraving on page 6 is from *The Animal Kingdom,* Hart Publishing Company, New York. The design motifs on pages 8, 10, 12, 80 are from the following books by Dover Publications, New York: *African Designs from Traditional Sources, American Indian Design and Decoration, Authentic Indian Designs, Decorative Art of the Southwestern Indians,* and *Design Motifs of Ancient Mexico.*

Front cover: *Bird with Flowers.* Italian. Inlay. *Office of Pietre Dure, Florence.*

Back cover: *Pair of ducks.* 19th century. Chinese. Embroidery, silk on silk. *Collection of Bruce Michel, New York.*

The display type for this book is Torino. The text face is Baskerville. The type was set at Filmtext, Inc. Color separations and halftones were made by National Colorgraphics, Inc. The text paper is 100 pound Warren Webflo, the cover is 10 point Warren Lusterkote, both supplied by Baldwin Paper Company. The book was printed and bound by Connecticut Printers, Inc.

Early 19th century. Engraving. From *Dictionary of Arts and Sciences*. William Nicholson. Mitchell, Ames, and White, Philadelphia, Pennsylvania.

CONTENTS

Early 19th century. Engraving. From *Dictionary of Arts and Sciences*. William Nicholson. Mitchell, Ames, and White, Philadelphia, Pennsylvania.

THE ARTFUL BIRD

From prehistory to the present, the bird in art has been endowed with a curious diversity of function and personality. In the hands of the artist, some have remained more or less birdlike–natural, biological creatures. But far more commonly, the illustrated bird has taken on one or more symbolic and man-centered roles, ranging from warrior to innocent, from traitor to moral guardian, from buffoon to divine messenger. Some of these roles have been only shortlived, the creations of a single artist or of a single period. Others–the dove as envoy of peace and tranquility, the hawk as a symbol of aggression, the domestic hen as the essence of maternity–have enjoyed a remarkable stability, over time.

The enviable capacity for flight is the quality that established the bird as an enduring symbol of freedom and independence and as an object of magic and mythology. A bird can reach the sky, and from there all things are possible. Many species, especially those that are high- or far-flying, have risen above the clouds to commune or even merge with the gods, and to share with them a certain capacity for shaping human destiny and environmental forces. The thunderbird, a hawk-like or eaglelike creation of the American Indian, was both a cause and a personification of violent electrical storms, and was feared and respected accordingly.

Above: *Springerle mold.* 1843. American. Carved wood, 8 in (20 cm) high. *Philadelphia Museum of Art.* Titus C. Geesey Collection.

Opposite: *Stories of St. Francis.* Detail, *Preaching to the Birds.* 15th century. Benozzo Gozzoli. Italian. Fresco. *San Francesco, Montefalco, Perugia, Italy.*

Several American Indian tribes revered the eagle itself, and ceremonially exhorted the bird to provide them with rain or to convey courage and power to their warriors. In the equally bird-involved culture of ancient Egypt, at least three gods were artistically represented as combination forms of men and birds. Ibises were often entombed with Egyptian royalty. The coming of a new pharaoh was heralded at the corners of the earth by four wild geese. The spirit of a deceased pharaoh was inclined to return to the site of its body's tomb in the form of a falcon. In ancient Greece, an eagle carried the thunderbolts of Zeus. In Rome, the same bird transported the souls of deceased emperors up to Mount Olympus.

Possessed of flight, birds have also been inspired to perform unique and compassionate acts on behalf of mankind. The dove obligingly returned to Noah with an olive branch, signaling the nearness of land to the storm-weary inmates of the ark. At the crucifixion, the finch alighted upon the cross to console Christ and to extract the nails from His limbs. (European medievals have pointed out that in the process, the bird pricked itself on a nail or thorn, as evidenced by the red plumage the bird now bears upon its breast.) In an equally humanitarian though carelessly executed maneuver, both the swallow and the wren singed their feathers while transporting sunlight from the heavens to earth, for use by mankind. The wren emerged from the venture with black, fire-caused streaks on

Right: *The Birds Enter the Ark (The Flood)*. Detail. 12th century. Italian. Mosaic. *St. Mark's, Venice.*

VOLVCRM/DISETIM/IDSEIEXOI
CASICPO

SSVSENOESCMChARDEHAPH

Above: *Construction*. 1921. Fernand Léger. French. Gouache, 19½ x 11 in (50 x 33 cm). *M. Knoedler and Company, New York.*

Right: *Bird in Space*. 1928 (?). Constantin Brancusi. Rumanian. Bronze (unique cast), 54 in (1.4 m) high. *Collection, The Museum of Modern Art, New York.* Given anonymously.

Opposite: *Twittering Machine*. 1922. Paul Klee. Swiss. Watercolor, pen and ink; 16¼ x 12 in (41 x 30 cm). *Collection, The Museum of Modern Art, New York.* Purchase.

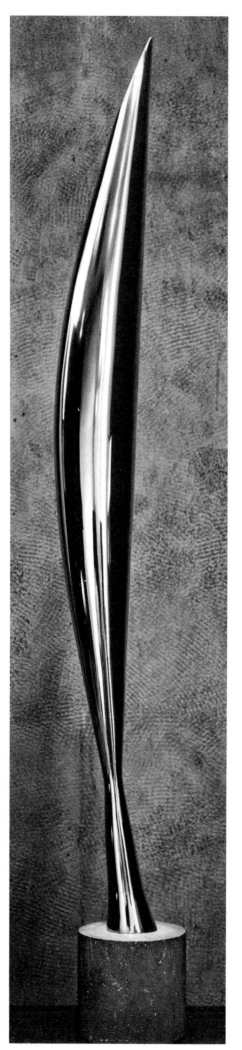

its plumage; the swallow had a sizeable, U-shaped portion of its tail feathers burned away.

In addition to flight, other unique or distinctive bird qualities have captured the eye and imagination of the artist or mythologist. Collectively, the egg-laying, nest-building, chick-sitting propensities have turned ducks, quail, hens, storks, and others into symbols of fertility, domesticity, and familial devotion. (At the same time, however, more cynical views of egg-laying and of other, originally reptilian characteristics have produced a small and somewhat bizarre sample of slithering, serpentine bird art.) Dramatic coloration also has helped establish the place of the bird in art. Sometimes this has been for the sake of symbolic in-nuendo—the eyes on the tail of the peacock or the mysterious blackness of the crow or raven—and sometimes for the sake of color alone. Conspicuous behavioral traits, too, such as the strength and warlike nature of birds of prey, the melodiousness of the thrush, the appar-ent naïveté of the gull in its indiscrimi-nate scavenging for food, and the garru-lous, nervous twittering and chirping of many smaller bird species, have all been captured in art and literature, sometimes respectfully or lovingly, sometimes with wrenching satire.

The perception of the bird world by mankind, and the reflection of this perception in art is an evolving process. We view birds far differently today than we did when they could soar higher and farther than we could. Our views of the bird are being changed profoundly by our technological and biological sophisti-cation, and by the uncomfortable aware-ness that we now hold the power to destroy our entire planetary environ-ment. While art, by definition, is never in complete harmony with our day-to-day perceptions, it is interesting to speculate on what forms the illustrated bird might take in the future.

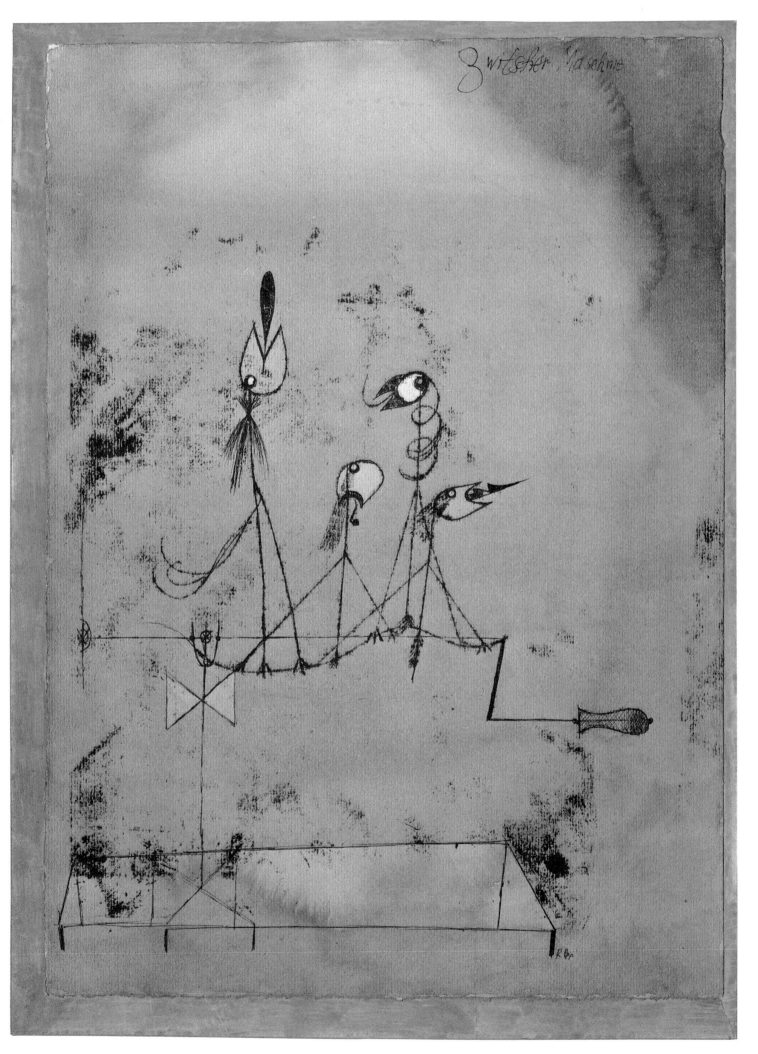

BITTERN

The hollow boom, boom, boom of the bittern echoes through the marshes and meadows. A master of camouflage, this heronlike bird hides among the tall reeds, without moving. Its brown body easily merges into its surroundings, while the white spots and streaks on its chest and throat look like rays of sunlight reflected off the water. Raising its beak to the sky, the bittern sways back and forth with the wind, defying detection.

Because it can be heard at night but is rarely seen, the bittern has always been considered one of the mysterious birds of the dark. Like the raven, its thundering voice is identified with evil tidings. If someone hears the bittern's cry, it is believed that bad luck is imminent. So rare are glimpses of the bittern that, even more than the crane, its flight has been associated with death. A popular folk saying in England advised, "If a bittern flies over your head, make your will." Perhaps the basis for this superstition comes from the adventures of a sportsman who shot down a bittern one cold winter and who within a few days found himself the victim of considerable misfortune. But another folktale suggests just the opposite: if a hunter wears a bittern's claw in the buttonhole of his jacket, it will bring good luck.

The bittern is popularly dubbed "stake driver" and "thunder pumper" because many people think its cry resembles the sound of a stake being driven into the ground or the noise of an old-fashioned hand pump. A common explanation for the sound is that the bittern thrusts his bill into a reed to make a low drumming call. However, the sound is probably caused by the bittern's rapid swallowing and ejecting of air.

Unlike herons and cranes, bitterns appear mostly at night, when they dine on insects, fish, and frogs. The bittern flies slowly through the air with its neck retracted and its head nestled against its shoulder. Bitterns have a heavier body and shorter neck than herons but the same thin, stiltlike legs. Experience has taught the bittern watchfulness and precaution. From the air they are easy prey for eagles, hawks, and owls; on the ground, they are hunted by water snakes and minks.

Right: *Nymph and Bittern.* 1809. William Rush. American. Bronze cast, 91 in (2.3m) high. For a fountain in Philadelphia. *Commissioners of Fairmount Park.*

Opposite: *Water Fowl.* 19th century. Chinese. Watercolor. *The Free Library of Philadelphia.*

BLUEBIRD

Above: *Bluebirds in Brushwood.* 19th century.
F. Bridges. American. Watercolor. *Kennedy Galleries, Inc., New York.*

Opposite: *Autour d'Elle.* Detail 1945. Marc Chagall. Russian. Oil on canvas. *Musée d'Arte Moderne, Paris.*

The sweet song and cheery presence of the bluebird in early spring are signals that the fury of winter is over. Since the bluebird is native only to North America, it was a stranger to the first European settlers in the New World. They named it, simply and appropriately, for its color.

Unlike other birds of the New World, such as the owl, turkey, or eagle, the bluebird was never given much prominence in the myths and legends of the American Indians, but it is featured frequently in American poetry and in popular songs. *The White Cliffs of Dover,* one of the great sentimental song hits of the World War II period, has lyrics describing the joys of lovers being reunited in peacetime when "There'll be bluebirds over the white cliffs of Dover…" This is more fanciful than factual since bluebirds are hardly likely to be found in England, but it does indicate the universal acceptance of the bluebird as a symbol of happiness. This symbolism can also be found in *The Bluebird,* a play written in 1909 by the Nobel Prize-winning Belgian poet and playwright, Maurice Maeterlinck. He had probably never seen a bluebird, and no one can be certain why he chose this particular bird. In the play, an allegorical fantasy, two small children set out to find the blue bird of happiness. Although the play ends with the blue bird eluding them, it did establish the bird as an enduring symbol of joy.

Bluebirds belong to the thrush family. There are three species: the eastern bluebird (which greeted the colonists), the western bluebird, and the mountain bluebird. The male mountain bird is uniformly blue in contrast to the blue-and-rust eastern bird. Bluebirds can be found in every state except Hawaii and in every Canadian province except Newfoundland. They are gentle creatures, easily intimidated by sparrows and starlings, but they can be scrappy fighters if threatened. Bluebirds are an asset on farms and in gardens since they live mostly on insects; wild berries provide the bulk of their winter food.

Plentiful at one time, bluebirds, particularly the eastern species, are decreasing in number almost to the point of becoming a legend. They are being pushed out of existence by human encroachment on their favorite habitats. In the city and country, dead trees with cavities that once provided nesting places are being cut down. Old wooden fence posts where the bluebird could find a cozy hollow have been replaced by metal posts. Bird lovers are now being encouraged to provide nesting boxes on their land in an effort to maintain the bluebird population.

CHICKEN

Above: *Rooster weathervane.* Mid-19th century. American (New York). Painted iron (cast body and sheet tail). Photo courtesy John Gordon Gallery.

Right: *Cock.* 20th century. Jacques Hnizdovsky. Ukrainian. Woodcut. From *The Animal Kingdom.* Hart Publishing Company, New York.

Opposite: *Cock Calling the Dawn.* 1923. Yasuo Kuniyoshi. American. Oil on canvas. *Columbus Gallery of Fine Arts, Ohio.* Gift of Ferdinand Howald.

Few bird couples are as different from each other as the hen and her mate, the proud cock. He struts through the barnyard as lord of the roost. He regally sounds his clarion at dawn to awaken everyone. In contrast to the rooster's majestic bearing, the earthy hen bustles through the yard followed by a brood of peeping chicks. Sitting on a nest or busily scratching for insects and seeds, she is the image of domestic toil.

From earliest times, many cultures have associated the cock with the sun. Not only does he announce the start of day, but his gleaming red crest appears to be a reflection of the sun's intense brightness. The ancient Greeks and Romans thus identified the cock with many of their solar gods. The Japanese believed that the cock's singing lured their sun goddess out from hiding. Even today roosters parade in front of Japan's great Shinto temples to remind people of this remarkable feat. In China when a man died, a cock was placed on top of his coffin as a symbol of his voyage beyond the sun.

For the Christians, however, the cock is a bird of augury, associated with Saint Peter's denial of Christ when, in warning, the cock crowed three times at dawn. According to another popular belief, the cock is the symbol of resurrection. It is said that one of the soldiers guarding Christ's tomb loudly denied that Christ would rise from the grave, declaring it was as unlikely as "the cock rising out of a boiling pot." No sooner had he uttered these words than the cock sprang from the pot. Metal and wooden roosters have since been placed on church steeples as a symbol of the resurrection.

As early as 1500 B.C., in India, roosters were trained to fight each other for sport. Down to this day, in several countries, many enjoy cockfighting despite laws against this cruel practice. So common was this spectacle during the eighteenth century that satirist William Hogarth portrayed cockfighting in engravings and included cockshying (throwing rocks at roosters) as one of *The Four Stages of Cruelty.*

Unlike her spouse, the hen has always had a more mundane image. She represents maternity, fertility, and domesticity. If a hen cackles loudly, many believe this means the owner's wife has too much authority, whence the common expression henpecked husband. When a red hen crows, some interpret this as a sign of fire; when a black hen crows, this is thought to indicate a theft. A white hen is seen as good luck. Perhaps the hen's greatest renown comes from her place in children's literature, especially as the wise red hen who planted, raised, and harvested the wheat in order to make bread while the cat, pig, and duck sat lazily by.

CRANE

Above: *Cranes.* Detail. Ancient Egyptian. Bas relief. Photo courtesy Egyptian Government Tourist Office, New York.

Opposite: *Mandarin Square.* Detail. Early Ming Dynasty. Chinese. Textile embroidery, silk on silk. *The Metropolitan Museum of Art, New York.* Fletcher Fund, 1936.

Slowly flying through the sky with its elegant long neck extended, wings outspread, and legs trailing behind, the crane looks like a magnificent flying cross. So impressive is this graceful soaring–whether a lone bird or a flock in V formation–that the crane has long been viewed as a bird of augury.

The ancient Greeks revered the crane as a guide to Hades, the immortal kingdom of the dead. According to legend, when the Greek poet Ibycus was murdered by unknown robbers, cranes pointed to the killers by mysteriously circling over the head of one of the guilty. In terror, the man cried out, "The cranes of Ibycus," henceforth a proverb for the avenging agents of the gods. Even today in America's rural south, many believe if a crane circles over a house three times, it means someone inside will die.

Many cultures have been enthralled by the crane's dancelike movements. In Japan and China crane dancers chased away evil spirits and communicated with the dead. After slaying the Minotaur, Theseus and his crew are said to have honored the sun with a crane dance, its gyrating movements reflecting the dark windings of the labyrinth.

The Chinese and Japanese, believing cranes lived thousands of years, used this bird in their art as a symbol of longevity. While Buddhists considered the crane a symbol of winter, elsewhere the bird was associated with fertility and the approach of

rain. In Christian literature, the crane became a symbol of good works. Russian, Indian, and Italian folktales picture the crane as a trickster, however; he invites fish to escape fishermen by riding to safety on his back, then quickly swallows his guests. The North American Indians told the story of a kindly old grandfather crane who helped runaways flee across the river by making a bridge with his long leg and who obligingly threw the runaways' pursuers in the water. Siberian legend recounts how the crane, angered by the quail, broke the latter's back so it would ever after fly close to the ground. The crane's haughty appearance and loud voice make it a perfect image for caricatures of high society.

Best known and largest of these bellowing birds is the whooping crane, named for its distinctive, coughlike whoop cry. Unfortunately the North American whooping crane is almost extinct. Thirteen other species, however, are common to North America, Mexico, Europe, Africa, India, and China. The food of the crane consists of all sorts of small animals and grains.

Cranes are frequently confused with herons, but unlike herons and bitterns, which fly with their heads nestled against their shoulders, cranes proudly extend their long necks in flight. This distinctive neck is forever remembered in the common expression "craning your neck."

CROW · RAVEN

No bird has occupied a more conspicuous place in fable, folklore, and literature than the crow. Since ancient times it has been both venerated and reviled, looked upon as a creature of supernatural powers, capable of spreading good fortune or creating havoc. Crows were believed by some to be associated with gods—or perhaps demons. Thus even though it was thought the birds could ward off bad spirits, there was always a chance that they might be demons themselves. Many of the superstitions about crows relate to their alleged ability to predict bad weather. They announce its imminence by their cries and the way they fly. A dead crow on the road was once considered a sign of good luck for the person who came upon it.

The crow has even become part of our everyday language: "as the crow flies" expresses the shortest distance between two points, and "to eat crow" is to be obliged to acknowledge that an opinion was held incorrectly.

The common crow is a partially migratory bird related to the raven, magpie, jay, rook, and jackdaw. The crow walks on the ground to feed and it is an omnivorous eater. It spurns little and particularly likes cultivated farming country (to which farmers whose fields have been raided by greedy crows will attest).

Raven is the common name for the largest member of the crow family. The glossy black scavenging bird's call is a guttural croak. It prefers wilderness areas, arctic coasts and barrens, and coniferous forests.

According to Roman legend, ravens were once as white as swans until one day a raven told Apollo that his beloved had been unfaithful to him. Apollo killed the bird's lover with a dart, but angered at the tattletale bird, he blackened its beautiful white feathers.

The raven first fluttered into favorable public notice when Noah released one from the Ark in company with a dove to learn in which direction land lay. The Vikings used it for the same purpose, and according to Norse legend, Iceland was discovered with the aid of ravens. The raven was highly regarded by ancient Norsemen because of its association with Odin, their chief god. A pair of ravens sat on Odin's shoulders and served as his messengers. Alexander the Great was said to have been guided across the desert by two ravens sent from heaven. The raven is also a symbol of benevolence in Christian art. It was a raven who fed the prophet Elijah in the wilderness and who saved Saint Benedict from eating poisonous food.

Regardless of their good or evil reputations, crows and ravens are considered the most intelligent of all birds. Easily trained, they can keep track of up to five or six objects and learn to repeat short sentences. The best proof of the birds' intelligence is the way they have managed to outwit humans and to profit from man's agricultural activities.

Today, a small flock of ravens lives in the Tower of London. Their well-being is a matter of concern to many, for tradition has it that the downfall of Britain will come when there are no more ravens in the Tower. Immortality is assured for the ebony-colored bird, however, because of the one who repeats the melancholy refrain, "Nevermore," in Edgar Allen Poe's famous poem, *The Raven*.

Above: *Blackbird on a vase*. Detail. 50 A.D. Fresco. Italian. *Casa degli Uccelli, Pompei.*

Opposite: Mother Hen with Chicks. 1968. Dragan Gazi. Yugoslavian. Oil on canvas. *Primitive Art Show, Zagreb, Yugoslavia.*

DOVE · PIGEON

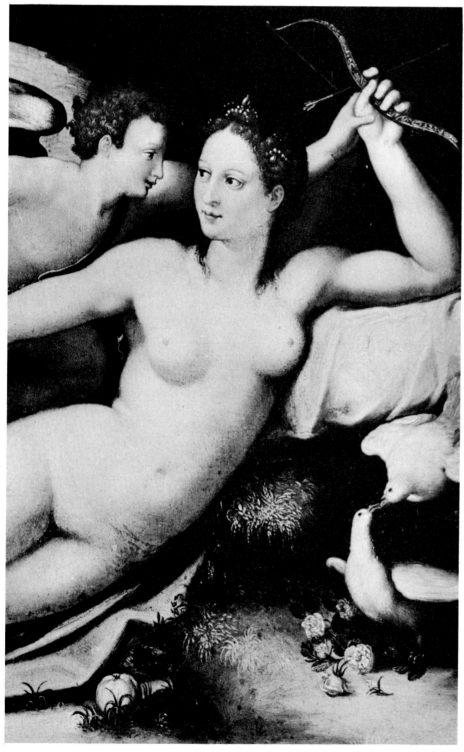

Top: 17th century. Joseph Crawhall. English. Woodcuts. From *Quaint Cuts in the Chapbook Style*. Dover Publications, New York.

Above: *Venere e Cupido*. Detail. Late 16th-early 17th century. Allori. Italian. Oil on wood. *Uffizi, Florence.*

Opposite: *Femmes à la colombe*. Detail. 20th century. Marie Laurencin. French. Oil on canvas. *Gallerie d'Art Moderne, Paris.*

Beginning with biblical times, when Noah sent the dove from the Ark and it returned with an olive leaf indicating that the flood waters were receding and that tranquility would be restored, the dove has been a symbol of peace and gentleness.

Its soft cooing call and amatory inclinations have long associated the dove with love and fecundity, and it was regarded as sacred to the goddesses who bestowed these special blessings. The dove had great religious significance for many of the early peoples. It was held sacred by the Phoenicians and Philistines. Turtledoves were offered in the temple by women after childbirth as a thanksgiving. An early belief that the dove was of divine origin was given further support by the theory that Satan could change himself into any animal he wished except the dove. All manner of portents were ascribed to the bird: prolonged cooing of the mourning dove heralded an end to drought; a white dove flying overhead was a good-luck omen; to dream of doves signified good health. According to *The Odyssey*, the dove carried messages for Zeus.

Even thousands of years ago, reverence for the dove did not interfere with widespread appreciation for the tasty morsel it provided when cooked. The Egyptians raised pigeons for food and probably to carry messages as early as 3000 B.C. At the original Olympic Games, homing pigeons were kept in readiness to be released to neighboring cities with the names of the winners. No one knows for certain when pigeons were first used as a means of communication in war, but Julius Caesar employed them to send word of his victories back to Rome.

There are about 300 species of doves and pigeons. The two terms are interchangeable, but dove is the older name and generally refers to the smaller members of the family. Some species are no bigger than a skylark and others are as large as a chicken. Pigeons are found in all parts of the world except the coldest regions. Their main food is fruits and seeds although city birds become scavengers. The most familiar pigeon is the rock dove. This is the bird city dwellers see mincing along with quick short steps, moving its head backward and forward and jerking its beautiful tail. Its ancestors, imported from England by pigeon fanciers, still breed on European sea cliffs. Today most cities have their self-perpetuating flocks of pigeons, which perhaps find the high stone buildings dimly reminiscent of their ancestral sea cliffs.

Above: *Mosaico di colombe*. Detail. Italian.
Column mosaic. *Musei Capitolini, Rome.*

Opposite: *Annunciation.* Detail. 15th century.
Filippo Lippi. Panel painting. *Galleria Doria,
Rome.*

DUCK

Whether waddling awkwardly across the ground on flapping webbed feet or paddling gracefully through the water, the duck has always evoked a happy, familiar image. It is a born comic, noisily quacking and bustling about in seemingly silly confusion. Every spring a fluffy contingent of peeping ducklings trails behind doting parents as a seasonal herald and a joy to watch.

In the Orient, where wild mandarin ducks are often seen swimming together, the duck is a symbol of the married couple. It represents fidelity, affection, and according to some Chinese legends, sexual prowess. On the wedding night, the bridal chamber is thus lovingly decorated with pictures of pairs of ducks. The Egyptians also revered the duck; pictures of swimming ducks in wildlife scenes were drawn on the walls of the pharaohs' tombs.

To the American Indian, the duck was the infallible guide of the earth, air, and water. Many tribes work duck feathers in ceremonial dances as a symbol of fertility and plenty. The Iroquois quacked noisily, and the Kutchin Indians flapped their arms about in imitation of the bird. During the 1920s many swinging boogie-woogie fanciers strutted and waddled in the duck-walk.

Everyone enjoys the legends, stories, and songs about the duck. A favorite Russian fairy tale by Afanassieff recounts the story of an evil witch who turned a lovely princess into a white duck when her husband was away. The poor duck, after laying three eggs, was eventually rescued by her husband, who grabbed his wife by the wings, uttered some magic words, and broke the spell. Another Eastern tale credits the duck with having laid the golden egg. And what child does not cherish Beatrix Potter's poor Jemima Puddle-Duck, who was in such a dither that she abandoned her nest full of eggs and never had ducklings of her own. Few other birds are as well known to people of all ages as is the duck, identified since earliest childhood as a friend.

Top: *Flying mallard.* Early 20th century. Elmer Crowell. American (Massachusetts). Carved and painted wood. Photo courtesy John Gordon Gallery.

Above: 19th century. Engraving. From *Old Engravings and Illustrations.* The Dick Sutphen Studio.

Opposite: *Pair of ducks.* Detail. 19th century. Chinese. Embroidery, silk on silk. *Collection of Bruce Michel, New York.*

EAGLE

Above: *Eagle holding snake.* Late 19th century. American (New England). Carved wood and gilt. Photo courtesy John Gordon Gallery.

Opposite: *Stylized bird.* Early 19th century. American (Pennsylvania). Stencil and watercolor. *The Metropolitan Museum of Art, New York.* Gift of Edgar William and Bernice Chrysler Garbisch, 1966.

Sitting motionless for hours on some commanding lookout or soaring effortlessly through the skies on broad, powerful wings, the eagle symbolizes all that is strong, courageous, free, and wild. Known as the king of birds and the bird of kings, the eagle has been an emblem of royal or imperial power for thousands of years.

To ancient Rome the eagle was a symbol of victory and was emblazoned on the standards its conquering legions carried. It was adopted as an imperial symbol by Russia and the Austro-Hungarian Empire and by France and Germany among other countries. Its prestige lives on in modern heraldry; today the bald eagle, native only to North America, is the national bird of the United States, depicted on the country's Great Seal.

The eagle has always been regarded with respect and reverence by many different cultures. Early Persian and Egyptian art shows the eagle with its talons sunk into a serpent or a dragon representing the triumph of good over evil. The ancient Greeks believed that the eagle was sacred to Zeus, god of the elements, and was the bearer of his thunderbolts. Peasants buried eagle wings in their fields as an offering to Zeus to protect their crops from damage by storms.

An eagle was always launched from the funeral pyre of a Roman emperor to carry his soul up to Olympus. There are many tales of eagles swooping down from the heavens as messengers of the gods to warn mortals of threatening disaster or to bring a gift of healing herbs. Some North American Indian tribes regarded the eagle almost

as a deity; only the bravest warriors were permitted to wear eagle feathers as rewards for their deeds. To invoke the rain gods the Zuñi of New Mexico used four eagle feathers to represent the four winds.

Members of the hawk family, eagles have the characteristic powerful talons and hooked bill for catching prey and tearing it to pieces. Both male and female eagles are devoted parents, building huge nests for their families high in trees or on cliffs, feeding their young industriously and fussing over their nestlings' first attempts at flight.

Found on almost all continents, eagles generally inhabit areas near water or high in mountains. Those living mainly near water supplement their favorite diet of fish with carrion, rodents, and small animals. They sometimes pirate the fish catch of other hawks in midair. The white-headed, white-tailed bald eagle belongs to this group. Its common name is derived from an old definition of bald meaning to have a white patch on the forehead. Eagles of the mountains and other rocky areas mainly live on young mammals. Of this group, the most widely seen in both North America and Eurasia is the golden eagle with its golden-brown neck feathers.

The eagle has become a victim of progress. There has been a marked decline in its population caused by people spreading out and encroaching on nesting and breeding sites. Chemical contamination of the eagles' food supplies has adversely affected their reproductive systems. Human predators, too, have taken their toll. One of the most honored of all birds is now rapidly diminishing in number.

FALCON

Above: *Horus.* Detail. Ancient Egyptian. Wall painting. Photo courtesy Egyptian Government Tourist Office, New York.

Opposite: *Robert Cheseman.* Detail. 1533. Hans Holbein. German. Oil on canvas. *Mauritshuis, The Hague.*

The lordly falcon is one of the swiftest birds in the world. With lightning speed the falcon strikes animals often far bigger than itself, breaking the victim's back with the force of its dive. Crane, pelican, duck, partridge, or grouse, no bird is immune to the falcon's blow. It is small wonder that the falcon has been glorified through the ages as the fiercest bird, rivaled only by the eagle.

As long ago as 2000 B.C., the Chinese learned to harness the falcon's fearful energy in a sport known as falconry. This popular hunting game flourished throughout the ancient kingdoms of Persia, India, Japan, and Arabia, and it is still practiced today. Falconry was the rage in western Europe from the Middle Ages through the seventeenth century; it was enjoyed by kings, nobles, and even ladies. Even Juliet wished to lure Romeo by imitating the gentle sound of the falconer's voice. Many an aristocrat posed for a portrait with a falcon perched peacefully on the wrist.

While the nobility amused themselves with falcons in sport, artists turned the bird into symbols of victory. Pictures abounded showing the falcon with its talons ripping into a wild hare, the falcon representing the triumph over flesh and the hare standing for defeated lust. Printers and bookmakers adopted the image of a hooded falcon as their emblem, using it to symbolize hope.

The image of the falcon as victor goes back even farther—to the ancient Egyptians who associated the falcon with many of their deities. Both the sky god Horus and the sun god Ra appear in the form of a falcon or as a falcon-headed man. Often sculptures of falcons with human heads were placed in the pharaoh's tomb because it was believed that the king's soul might visit his mummified body in the shape of a falcon.

Members of the hawk family, falcons range in size from the falconet, that is no longer than a man's hand, to the large gyrfalcon. The birds are found in all parts of the world except Antarctica. Because the female is larger than the male, she is sometimes preferred for falconry. Unlike other hawks, falcons do not build their own nests, but lay eggs on the ground, cliffs, or ledges, or take over the abandoned nests of crows and hawks.

The number of falcons is rapidly declining in Europe and the United States, however, where the effects of the insecticide DDT has made the falcon's egg shells so brittle they often break before hatching. With painstaking care conservationists and ornithologists are slowly reversing this trend. Hopefully, someday this regal bird will once more reign in the wilderness.

MAN
M .

. ETATIS . SVÆ . X
M . D . XXXIII

33

Above: *Falconry.* Engraving. From *Deutsche Geschichte.* Ludwig Stacke. Velhagen and Klasing, Leipzig, Germany.

Opposite: *Très riches Heures du duc de Berry.* Detail. Early 15th century. Paul of Limburg.

Flemish. Illuminated manuscript. *Musée Condé, Chantilly.*

FINCH

Above: *Still Life with Two Goldfinch.* 1620. Balthasar Van Der Ast. Dutch. Oil, 11½ x 8½ in (29 x 21 cm). *The Fine Arts Gallery of San Diego, California.*

Opposite: *Madonna of the Goldfinch.* Detail. 18th century. Giovanni Battista Tiepolo. Italian. Oil. *National Gallery of Art, Washington, D.C.* Samuel H. Kress Collection.

The brightly colored finch is a merry songster. With its stout beak raised to the sky and plump breast swelling, the finch gaily twitters and chirps as it hops from tree to bush in search of seeds. Its decorative multicolored plumage–yellow, red, purple, brown, or white–has made it a favorite subject for artists throughout the centuries.

During the Middle Ages and Renaissance, when many paintings were devoted to religious themes, the goldfinch was used as a symbol of the crucifixion. Legend explained how the merciful finch, upon seeing Christ on the cross, flew down to console the Savior and wounded itself on a thorn in the Savior's crown. Forever after, the finch wore a red badge on his breast as a symbol of compassion. According to another tale, the finch ripped its small breast trying to pull the nails from the cross. The bird's diet of thorns and thistles was interpreted as a further sign of its suffering for Christ.

In hundreds of paintings of the Madonna and Child, the Infant Jesus appears holding a goldfinch in his tiny hand as an indication of the agony of the cross. It is said that a group of children visited the Infant Jesus bringing him clay birds as presents. As soon as the Infant touched the toy birds, their delicate wings began to flutter. The clay collection came to life, filling the air with joyful song. By the eighteenth century, however, the finch had lost some of this religious significance, appearing in numerous pastoral paintings merely for the bird's pleasing colors.

Finches are one of the largest bird families, common to all parts of the world except Australia. Often named for the color of the male, the most familiar species include the goldfinch, greenfinch, purplefinch, scarlet rosefinch, chaffinch, and bullfinch. The female bird is usually a softer, duller color.

Finch songs vary greatly according to their different species. So exceptional are many of these voices that finches were often kept as caged birds during the nineteenth century in Europe. Many poets bemoaned the fate of these caged creatures in their verse. Shelley compassionately wrote:

Poor captive bird! who from thy narrow cage,
Pourest such music, that it might assuage
The rugged hearts of those who prisoned thee
Were they not deaf to all sweet melody.

Fortunately, today finches are left to roam freely, where their delightful songs and colorful presence may be enjoyed by all.

GOOSE

Above: *Right and Left*. Late 19th century. Winslow Homer. American. Oil. *National Gallery of Art, Washington, D.C.* Gift of the Avalon Foundation.

Opposite: *Wild Geese*. 19th century. Chinese. Watercolor. *The Free Library of Philadelphia*.

Wild bird or domestic fowl, the goose is a long-time favorite of myth and folktale. Over 4,000 years ago, the Egyptians worshipped a goose-headed deity named Geb as their god of the earth. Egyptians believed that at death, the pharaoh's soul took the form of a goose. Each time a new pharaoh came to the throne, four wild geese were tossed in the air to announce the pharaoh's reign to the four corners of the horizon.

Hera, Greek goddess of fertility (later renamed Juno by the Romans), had the goose as her symbol. When the Gauls attacked Rome in the fourth century B.C., sacred geese in the Temple of Juno sounded the alarm and awakened the sleeping citizens with their loud cackling. Afterwards, each year, in honor of their bravery, the Romans marched through the streets carrying a golden goose.

Many cultures saw the goose as the divine steed of the gods. Hindu mythology pictures Brahma riding on the back of a splendid gander, the male of the species, the symbol of spiritual purity. Today when the Indian yogi chants *hamsa, hamsa* (the Hindu word for gander), he is trying to achieve cosmic freedom by awakening this inner purity. In China, where the goose is a symbol of conjugal fidelity, newlyweds re-

ceive a pair of geese as a wedding gift.

During the Middle Ages, people connected geese with witches, who were believed to ride the geese through the skies. Despite this association, the medieval English found no wrong in feasting on goose for Saint Michael's Day, when as part of their land rent, farmers presented a goose "fit for a lord." Down to this day, the English eat goose for that holiday.

But if the goose will live forever in legend, it is through the Grimm Brothers' *The Golden Goose* and Aesop's *The Goose that Laid the Golden Egg*, two fables based on the idea that the goose brings good luck to the innocent and disaster to the greedy. In the Grimms' story, each time thieves try to steal the golden feathers, the robbers cannot let go and are forced to hang on as the goose's simpleton owner moves onward. Eventually the simpleton leads this absurd procession to the king, makes the princess laugh, and thus wins her in marriage. In a Hindu variation, the Brahmin's wife plucks out all the golden feathers only to find them worthless. The foolish owner of Aesop's goose kills his prize in hopes of finding more gold inside. And who can forget the Grande Dame of all childhood nursery rhymes, Mother Goose?

GULL

From distant seas to inland lakes, rivers, and marshes, the gull is a ubiquitous water bird known as a wanderer. Trailing behind ships, circling over the water, or perched atop a harbor mooring, it is the universal emblem of the sea. Both adventurer and peaceful drifter, the gull can fly for miles with powerful, broad wings, or rock contentedly on the water, lulled by the tide.

Through the centuries, sailors have feared gulls, believing the souls of drowned sea mates live on in these birds. When three gulls flew overhead, sailors thought death would follow. So strong was this superstition that many a sailor immediately withdrew to his bed and died. Similarly many people felt that when a gull alighted on a house, it heralded bad luck. Yet no one dared harm them because killing a gull was sure to bring misfortune.

Despite these doomsday predictions elsewhere, the gull is a local hero in Salt Lake City, Utah, where it is honored with a grandiose marble monument. When the Mormons first settled in Salt Lake City in 1848, a massive swarm of flying black insects suddenly descended on their crops. The settlers fell to their knees in prayer. Miraculously, thousands of gulls appeared and, like a liberating army, attacked the insects thus saving the crops, hence the Mormons from starvation.

According to Indian legend in British Columbia, the gull was the first owner of daylight, which it selfishly guarded for its own use. One day the crafty crow broke open the gull's treasure box, releasing the gift of light for the benefit of all.

Although most of the old-time superstitions are now regarded as interesting myths, the gull is still highly regarded as a weather forecaster. When gulls fly inland, local wise men predict rain. Indeed, there is much to support this folk wisdom since gulls, unable to find fish in stormy weather, often fly to shore in search of insects.

Although often easily fooled, whence the English word "gullible," they fly fearlessly through hurricanes and can adjust to cold icebergs or warm tropics. Clad mostly in white with gray or black on its wings and back, the gull scans the water and shore for fish and mollusks. It will dash a shell against a rock with joyous shrieks, fly down to inspect the progress, then repeat this action three or four times before devouring the prize. These avid scavengers have so adapted to modern times that they are now as common at the local dump as on the ocean. In fact their growing population has become a problem in some areas where authorities seek ways of curtailing their proliferation.

Above: *Sperm Whaling in the South Pacific.* ca. 1825. American. Scrimshaw, engraved whale's tooth; 7¼ in (18 cm) long. Found in Nantucket, Massachusetts. *Collection of Barbara Johnson, New Jersey.*

Opposite: *They Wait.* 20th century. Zoltan Sepeshy. Tempera on masonite panel, 20 x 30 in (51 x 76 cm). *Nelson Gallery-Atkins Museum, Kansas City, Missouri.* Gift of Mrs. Jesse Raymond Battenfeld through the Battenfeld Foundation in memory of Jesse Battenfeld.

HERON

"The ill-omened heron doth Chalcedon
scourge with hate:
Why always traitor-bird 'tis called, let
Phoebus state,
When in the shallow sea, standing on its slim
legs
And pecking up food from out the sandy
dregs,
There to the city crossed from opposite the foe,
Having seen that through the shoal 'twas pos-
sible to go.
Stone the bad bird, for it from the enemy full
meed
Obtained, the traiter-fowl—both conches and
sea-weed.

The knights of medieval Europe hunted herons with falcons. The latter, though smaller than herons, are able to attack and overcome them from above and behind. Heron was served as the main course at the knights' banquets; the appearance of the cooked heron at the table was a signal to the knights to begin a round of boasting about their adventures and the skill of their favorite falcons.

The name heron, which means "to utter sharp cries," developed from an old German name for the birds—*heiger.* At various times and in various parts of Europe, the heron has been called *hairon, hern, heronceau,* and *hernshaw.* Herons are wading birds that eat mostly fish, but also small amphibians, mammals, and sometimes even other birds. There are about 60 different species of heron. Short-legged herons search for food in shallow water, while their longer-legged cousins prefer food found in deeper water. Thus, overcrowding is avoided, although herons are gregarious, tending to congregate both with each other and with other wading birds such as egrets, storks, and ibises.

Both male and female herons are large birds: gray, blue, brown, or white, streaked, and barred. During the mating season males may develop colorful skin on their foreheads or elongated plumes on their heads, necks, breasts, and backs.

In flight a heron is easily distinguished from other birds by its characteristic body position—its neck is held in an S shape and its legs float straight out behind like streamers in the wind.

Above: *Aztatl.* Mexico. Clay stamp. From *Design Motifs of Ancient Mexico.* Jorge Enciso. Dover Publications, New York.

Opposite: *The Hunt of the Unicorn IV.* Detail. Late 15th century. Franco-Flemish. Textile tapestry; silk and wool with silver and silver-gilt threads. *The Cloisters Collection of the Metropolitan Museum of Art, New York.* Gift of John D. Rockefeller, Jr., 1937.

Although found in most parts of the world, herons are particularly special to North Americans. The American writer Henry Thoreau even suggested making them United States citizens. Though never officially granted such status, herons appeared on a 1947 United States postage stamp—the first bird ever to be so honored solely because of its distinctive appearance. (Bald eagles were once pictured because of their role as an official symbol of the United States.)

Yet herons have not always been so highly thought of throughout history. In the Bible (King James Version, Leviticus 11 and Deuteronomy 14) Moses declared herons to be taboo as food. Antipholus of ancient Greece described herons as traitor-birds because they waded in shallow salt-water areas and thus alerted the Greeks' enemies to good landing spots:

HUMMINGBIRD

Despite the name, none of the over 300 known species of hummingbird is especially talented musically. The bird creates a hum by extraordinarily fast wing flapping–sometimes as fast as 200 beats per second but more often in the range of 25 to 30 beats. The hum can be so loud that the Indians of British Columbia called it miniature thunder.

Strictly native to the Western Hemisphere, hummingbirds hail mostly from South America, especially Brazil and Equador. They are considered good luck in much of Latin America. In Costa Rica for example, where hummingbirds are called *rey de los garriones,* "king of the sparrows," believers will climb very tall trees to obtain the nests to carry as amulets. The knowledge of and fascination with hummingbirds is centuries old. In the 1700s Father Bernabe Cobo taught Chilean natives about Jesus Christ's resurrection by comparing it to the hummingbird's extraordinary ability to go into a torpid, deathlike state during brief cold spells, returning to normality when the temperature rises.

Some hummingbirds migrate from Central America to North America each year with the seasons. It is not yet known just how far hummingbirds can fly at a stretch. It is known, however, that hummingbirds possess unsurpassed flying agility. Helicopterlike, they can hold steady in space or fly forwards, backwards, and sideways; like the stunt pilot, they can fly upside down and stop on a dime. Unlike other birds, the hummingbird's wings beat back and forth rather than up and down, thus they get twice the power from a single flap of the wings.

The hummingbird's flying speed is also exceptional. This was described by the poet Jones Very:

Like thoughts that flit across the mind
Leaving no lasting trace behind
The hummingbird darts to and fro
Comes, vanishes before we know.

The speed is also acknowledged in the French name for hummingbirds, *oiseaux-mouches,* "birds like flies."

Their speed is not the only reason hummingbirds are hard to spot, despite their brilliant, jewellike colors. These glittering fragments of the rainbow, as Audubon called them, are very tiny fragments indeed. The bee hummingbird grows no longer than a chicken egg. The nests, too, are very tiny–often the size of a large walnut.

Never tell anyone that he or she has the appetite of a hummingbird. If that person did, he would eat two or three times his weight of food a day. Hummingbirds eat all day long to replace the energy used in flying; small insects and flower nectar make up their meals.

Because they are most often seen while visiting brightly colored garden flowers for nectar, the Spanish name for hummingbirds is *pica flor,* "flower picker," and the Portuguese name is *beija flor,* "flower kisser." Though hummingbirds are in reality fun loving and often feisty, their own beauty and that of the flowers they flit among, evoke an image of delicate beauty to those who get only a glimpse of them.

Above: *Huitzizillin.* Yucatan. Clay stamp. From *Design Motifs of Ancient Mexico.* Jorge Enciso. Dover Publications, New York.

Below: *Huitziloxochitl.* Mexico City. Clay stamp. From *Design Motifs of Ancient Mexico.* Jorge Enciso. Dover Publications, New York.

Opposite: *Passion Flowers and Hummingbirds.* 19th century. Martin Johnson Heade. American. Oil on canvas. *Museum of Fine Arts, Boston, Massachusetts.* M. and M. Karolik Collection.

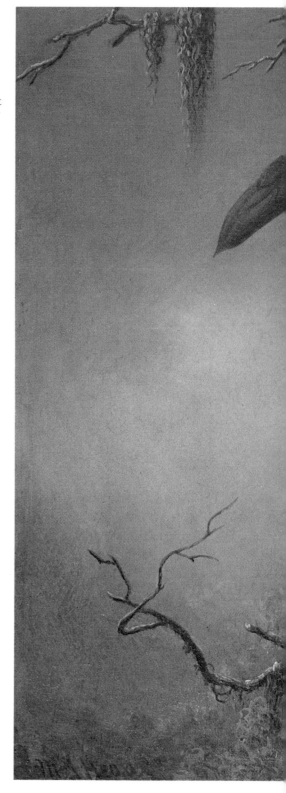

IBIS

No bird has been more revered than was the ibis in ancient Egypt. Considered sacred, mummified remains of ibises have been found in many royal Egyptian tombs next to the gold, jewels, and other treasures. The reason for this veneration was the ibis's relationship to Thoth, the scribe or secretary of the gods (especially the god, Osiris). Thoth's name, written in hieroglyphics, was a picture of the ibis.

It is not known just how the ibis first got into the cities of ancient Egypt as it is thought the bird was not indigenous to these areas. Most likely the first birds were captured and brought back from the shores of the Red Sea. In any case, the reverent protection given the birds allowed them to multiply to great numbers.

Later the birds disappeared from Egypt. Again, it is not known why or when the ibis disappeared, but it is known that there were ibises in Egypt at the time of the Roman conquest and that returning Romans introduced the birds into Italy.

It was the white ibis that the ancient Egyptians favored, but there are at least 30 species of different colors with some species found on each of the five major continents. Related to storks, herons, and spoonbills, the ibis has the long, thin legs and straight or curved bills suitable for marsh-loving birds. Water and the ibis go together–the bird can be found wading in tropical lagoons, coastal shallows, mud flats, and flooded rice fields. Only occasionally does it wander a few miles inland to nest in forests and pastoral lands.

Generally, ibises eat small crustaceans, mollusks, fish, and young, tender plants. One species eats insects; some eat snakes. In captivity ibises often eat a wider range of foods than in the wild.

Ibises are naturally gregarious birds; colonies meet together in the breeding season for great discussions in both harsh or muted voices, depending on the species. Nests are built of twigs, and two to five eggs are laid. Some species' nests are constructed high above the ground, while other species nest down low.

Ups and downs in the population of ibises seem to be their destiny. In some parts of the world, ibises have been and are eaten by humans; other ibises have been nearly exterminated at times by plume hunters, but so far wildlife conservationists' efforts have managed to save the birds from extinction.

Above: *Figure of a sacred ibis.* 332–30 B.C. Egyptian. Bronze and wood covered with linen and gesso, 13¼ x 5¼ x 17 in (34 x 13 x 43 cm). *The Metropolitan Museum of Art, New York.* The Harris Brisbane Dick Fund, 1955.

Right: *The Sacred Ibis.* 19th century. Engraving. From *Johnson's Natural History.* S.G. Goodrich and A. Winchell. A.J. Johnson, New York.

Opposite: *Arm panel of throne of Thut-mose IV.* 1420 B.C. Egyptian. Sculpture relief on cedar, 9¾ in (25 cm) high. *The Metropolitan Museum of Art, New York.* The Theodore M. Davis Collection. Bequest of Theodore M. Davis, 1915.

47

MAGPIE

Above: *Nativity*. Detail. Late 15th century. Piero della Francesca. Italian. *National Gallery, London.*

Below: Engraving. From *The New Natural History*. Richard Lydekker. Merrill and Baker, New York.

Opposite: *Don Manuel Osorio de Zuñiga*. Detail. 1784. Francisco de Goya. Spanish. Oil on canvas. *The Metropolitan Museum of Art, New York.* The Jules S. Bache Collection, 1949.

The magpie is conspicuous for its noisy chattering and its striking black and white plumage, which is set off with a blue wing patch and a long wedge-shaped tail stroked with green. Gregarious birds rarely traveling alone, they are generally seen in flocks, walking along in the open country searching for grasshoppers or beetles, and jabbering away like a group of light-hearted children just let out of school.

The magpie is about the size of a small crow, to which it is related. If not molested, magpies are friendly and will become frequent visitors around farm or ranch buildings. They can be trained as pets and taught to imitate some words. Magpies are not at all discriminating about food; they will eat almost anything from large insects to carrion and waste grain. In the early days of America, they would wait around Indian camps for anything edible and trail behind buffalo hunters to pick up refuse from the hunt.

The most common species is the black-billed magpie. Its scientific name is *Pica pica*, which led to its being known as the pie bird. The British called the pie bird Mag, short for Margaret, and from this combination of words evolved magpie.

Magpies are notorious thieves. They will pick up any bright objects they can lift and carry them off to their nests to add to their hoard. The nests are large domed structures with openings in both sides and are built in the forks of trees. Their incredibly sloppy housekeeping practices have given rise to the figure of speech "untidy as a magpie's nest." People who talk too much or have thievish tendencies are unflatteringly called magpies. But the term was also used irreverently for members of the English clergy who wore black and white clothing. Some etymologists believe that the pie we eat was named for the magpie because its filling is as untidy and disordered as a magpie's nest.

In times past, country people living in the British Isles considered the magpie sinister and possessed of evil powers. A magpie's flight past a window was a portent of a death in the household. It may be that the bird's black and white plumage and its association with ravens and other birds that gather around dead carcasses nourished these suspicions. However, the people had ways of dealing with the magpie's evil and of dispelling its mischief. On meeting the bird, they could cross their thumbs and say:

I cross the magpie, the magpie crosses me,
Bad luck to the magpie and good luck to me.

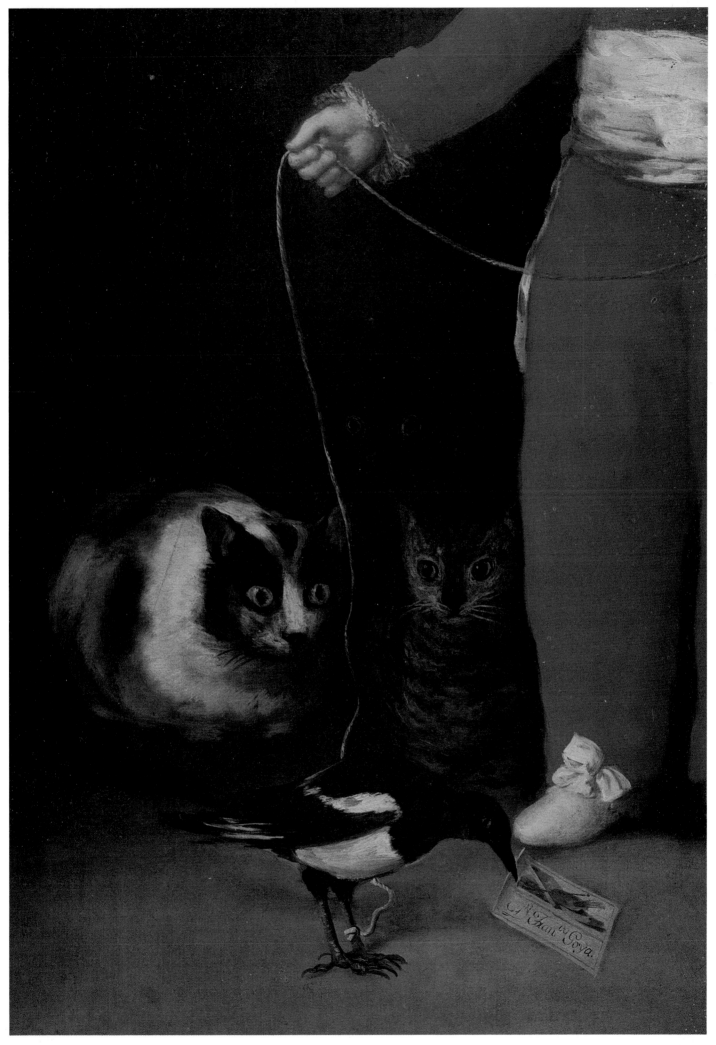

OSTRICH

The biggest birds on earth, ostriches, are gawky looking because of their thin legs, egg-shaped bodies, and long snaky necks. Male ostriches are strikingly beautiful with coal-black feathers and contrasting snow-white wing tips and tail plumes. Females are shorter, weigh slightly less, and have brown feathers.

Ostriches, like penguins, cannot fly. They move about by walking or running. When frightened, they can run extremely fast. Because of their running ability and their keen vision, which aids in early detection of enemies, ostriches can often escape natural dangers.

Man has hunted ostriches since very early in history. At least one Neolithic rock carving shows a man pointing an arrow at an ostrich. Later hunters learned they could easily get close to ostriches by disguising themselves in ostrich feathers. The hunt was made easier because of the fact that once the bird detected the hunter, the bird would run panic-stricken in circles rather than away from the hunter.

It may have been this trait of circling when frightened that led to the belief that ostriches are stupid. Or it may have been the rather scatter-brained expression on their faces. It was probably this belief that led an early Greek, Julius Antecessor, to say to an acquaintance,

Like ostrich's thy face! Has Circe stirred
For thee some potion, which made thee a bird?"

In fact, ostriches are neither more nor less intelligent than other birds.

Another persistent myth is that ostriches bury their heads in sand when disturbed. They do not. This story probably arose because nesting ostriches will lay their heads on the ground to hide from enemies rather than to abandon their ground-level nests.

Ostrich eggs are edible. As food, they equal about 24 chicken eggs. Fragments of ostrich eggs have been found in archeological digs tracing very early societies in both North Africa and China, although wild ostriches are found today only in Africa.

It is certain that the ancient Egyptians, Arabians, Indians, and Greeks were all familiar with ostriches. They were sometimes kept as pets for rulers though

the birds were never truly domesticated. Ostriches were used for chariot racing, despite their stubborn habit of sitting down and refusing to budge when tired.

Early warriors wore ostrich plumes as symbols of heroism and three ostrich plumes still top the Prince of Wales' emblem. Later in history, women adopted ostrich plumes as hat decorations, and ostrich skin was favored for leather gloves and purses. Ostrich plumes became so fashionable in the late nineteenth century that ostrich farms sprang up in Africa, Australia, and the United States.

If you see an ostrich, don't try to get too close. The bird can injure or kill you just by kicking, if prevented from running away. Ostriches are best admired from a distance as they're big enough to see from far away.

Above: *L'Autruche.* 1867. French. Engraving. From *La Vie Parisienne.* Paris.

Opposite: *Dopo il diluvio universale.* Detail. F. Palizzi. Italian. *Capodimonte, Naples.*

OWL

Above: *Owl.* January 20, 1947. Pablo Picasso. Spanish. Lithograph, printed in black and yellow ochre, 25 ½ x 19 ½ in (65 x 49 cm). *Collection, The Museum of Modern Art, New York.* Curt Valentin Bequest.

Opposite: *Garden of Earthly Delights.* Detail, center panel. Late 15th century. Hieronymus Bosch. Dutch. Oil on wood. *Prado, Madrid.*

Clad in soft, fluffy plumage that makes it almost noiseless in flight and with eyes that can see in the dark, the owl is a bird of night, hunting its prey in darkness. So identified is it with the waning light of the day that twilight has been called owl light. Because of its nocturnal activity, grave expression, and strange, haunting call, the owl has long been associated with mystery and magic, occupying a prominent place in mythology and folklore.

There were so many owls in ancient Athens that a saying of the time, "To send owls to Athens," was the equivalent of the present-day, "To carry coals to Newcastle," which implies taking something to where it is already plentiful. The Greeks made the owl sacred to Athena, the goddess of wisdom, which probably was the basis for the owl's great–and greatly overrated– reputation for being the wisest of birds. Actually, owls are easily fooled. But the Greeks considered them birds of prophecy –portents of evil as well as of triumph, depending upon the circumstances of their appearance.

The stigma of evil and supernatural power persisted through the centuries. Many people have feared the bird, some believing that the owl's cry foretold death and disaster. But since owls shared a fellowship with demons and witches, it was believed that they also had the power to ward off other bad spirits. For protection against lightning, the Chinese placed figures of owls on rooftops, and in Germany real owls were attached to doors.

All owls have hooked beaks and powerful feet with talons for catching and holding prey. They will dine off rodents, snakes, and insects; some catch fish. The bigger the owl, the bigger the animal it preys on. The owl's particular fondness for mice has won it the special appreciation of farmers.

The sound most often associated with owls is the soft deep *hoo* sound. There are over a hundred species of owls found all over the world, and each has its own distinctive sound, ranging from a wail to a cackle, a cluck, a high-pitched bell sound, and a low-pitched toot.

The owl has been a favorite subject of sculptors, artists, and poets since earliest times. Its likeness has appeared on ancient coins and in Renaissance paintings. Chaucer, Shakespeare, Ben Jonson, Thomas Gray, and other writers have alluded to it in their works, but it took the delightful nonsense rhymes of Edward Lear to give the owl literary immortality. What child has not responded to the lilting rhythm of *The Owl and the Pussycat* in which these two splendid creatures sail away for a year and a day to the land where the Bong-tree grows?

PARROT

The chattering, gaudy-hued parrot has always intrigued people. Native to the tropics, it brings color and sound to forests and deep jungles as it flies through the air, shrieking and squawking. Like most talking birds, though, the parrot cannot sing.

Some species can be bred in captivity, and for thousands of years parrots have been popular as caged birds, acting as willing models for artists who wish to draw them from life. In ancient India, the parrot had the same sensual significance as the goose and was often pictured being ridden through the skies by the god of love.

Parrots are among the most intelligent and adaptable of birds, but some of the extraordinary feats of speech attributed to them are, no doubt, exaggerated. There was an early belief, never substantiated, that parrots could predict weather. It was thought that loud parrot squawking, for example, meant it was going to rain.

There is a tale of an ancient parrot that had been reared in a South American tribe. After the tribe became extinct, the parrot remained the last creature on earth to use the language. A story from an eighteenth-century writer tells of a gray parrot that was purchased by a cardinal of the church because the bird could recite the Apostle's Creed without an error. It was said this same bird dreamed aloud.

Wild parrots are found in South and Central America, southern Africa, India, Southeast Asia, Australia, New Zealand, and other Pacific Islands. The macaws are the largest members of the parrot family, which numbers over 300 living species. Parrots are the best climbers among birds. Two of their thick curving toes point forward and two point backward, giving them a strong grasp on a branch. They use their bills as a third foot to pull themselves along. These flint-hard bills are perfectly designed for the job of gouging, cracking, or hammering nuts or other hard objects. Parrots are unusually dexterous, able to use their feet like hands to grasp food while eating. They may be left footed or right footed.

Parrots have many winning qualities. While they can sometimes be moody and mischievous, domesticated parrots are usually affectionate and eager to please. There is little evidence to support the belief that the parrot knows what it is saying. It merely associates phrases with particular people and situations. Thus, the statement that "Polly wants a cracker" does not mean that Polly is really hungry.

Above: *Fraktur drawing with parrot.* Early 18th century. Heinrich Otto. American (Pennsylvania). Ink and watercolor on paper. Photo courtesy John Gordon Gallery.

Right: From *American Indian Design and Decoration.* LeRoy Appleton. Dover Publications, New York.

Opposite: *Lady With Her Pets.* Detail. Early 19th century. Rufus Hathaway. American. Oil on canvas. *The Metropolitan Museum of Art, New York.* Gift of Edgar William and Bernice Chrysler Garbisch, 1963.

PEACOCK

Above: From *Chinese Cut-Paper Designs.* Selected by Theodore Menten. Dover Publications, New York.

Right: 17th century. Joseph Crawhill. English. Woodcut. From *Quaint Cuts in the Chapbook Style.* Dover Publications, New York.

Opposite: *Peacocks.* Detail. 1683. Melchior D'Hondecoeter. Dutch. Oil on canvas. *The Metropolitan Museum of Art, New York.* Gift of Samuel H. Kress, 1927.

The magnificently endowed peacock has posed and strutted in the gardens of kings and emperors during biblical times and before and has attracted attention throughout the world ever since. When he raises the feathered train high above his back, rattles his quills, and emits raucous, harsh screams, he is unsurpassed for drama and beauty. Although this display is part of the peacock's courtship ritual (small wonder that peacocks have harems of two to five hens), he will not hesitate to repeat the performance for attentive humans.

According to ancient Greek legend, the peacock was sacred to the goddess Hera. She directed Argus, the creature with 100 eyes, to spy on a rival. When Argus was slain, Hera placed his eyes on the tail of her favorite bird. One of the earliest mentions of peacocks in literature was in the play *The Birds,* written by Aristophanes in 414 B.C. Early Christians are believed to have used the peacock to symbolize the resurrection of the body of Christ and the immortality of the soul.

Indian artists depicted various Hindu deities being borne through the air or riding on the backs of the birds. The feathers worked into embroidery were often used in early church decorations. In China, the feathers were valued higly during the T'ang dynasty over 1,000 years ago. Districts paid their taxes with peacocks because the feathers were needed as decorations during royal processions, and they were also presented to officials as rewards for loyal and faithful service.

Peafowl (the generic name for the male peacock and the female peahen) are members of the same family as pheasants, grouse, and turkeys. Before the turkey became widely known, peacocks were often served at banquets, complete with gilded head and tail feathers.

Although unable to fly long distances, peafowl can quickly break into strong, short bursts of flight; in addition, they are good runners. Scratching their food from the ground, peafowl are content to eat anything from grains and seeds to small insects. At night they seek safe roosts high in trees. The blue, or common, peafowl originated in India and Ceylon (now Sri Lanka) and has been domesticated for over 2,000 years. It has adapted readily to many parts of the world and graces gardens today much as it has for centuries.

Opposite: Poster reproduction of *Bradley His Book.* 1924. William Bradley. American. Wood engraving in color. *From the collection of Henry Lawrence Sparks.* Printed in the 1924 Craftsmen Number of *The American Printer.* Edgar C. Ruwe Company, New York.

Above: *Dutch decorative panel.* June 1939. *School Arts Magazine.* Worcester, Massachusetts.

PELICAN

During medieval times the pelican was a symbol in Christian art of self-sacrifice and charity. An emblem showing a stylized pelican bending over chicks that were huddled beneath her breast appeared often in church windows and sculptures. The emblem was called "a pelican in her piety," piety having the classical meaning of filial devotion. This concept grew out of a belief current at the time that the pelican wounded her own breast with her bill and restored her ailing young with her blood. This fallacious belief arose from the fact that pelicans feed their young with their own partly digested stomach contents. The hungry babies thrust their heads down the parent's gullet and gobble up the predigested food. Uninformed fishermen watching the feeding procedure from a distance may have thought that the nestlings were sucking the parent's blood, particularly if the fishermen saw the parent birds then preening their breast feathers with their beaks—a necessary procedure for the pelicans to coat their feathers with oil.

After it became a symbol of self-sacrifice, the pelican was mentioned frequently in poetry and plays. Shakespeare refers to the pelican as a symbol of concern for others in a number of his plays. King Lear, for example, speaks of his "pelican daughters." A character in *Love for Love* by William Congreve, the seventeenth-century English dramatist says, "What, wouldst thou have me turn pelican and feed thee out of my vitals?"

Pelicans are found on inland lakes and along ocean coastlines of North and South America, as well as in parts of Europe, Asia, Africa, and Australia. Coloring may be brown, black and white, white, or white tinged with pink. Fishing techniques vary among the different species. The brown pelican sights a fish from the air and dives in nose first, disappearing under the water to catch the prey, then surfacing tail first. The white pelican, in contrast, scoops the fish into its mouth as it swims. Sometimes the pelican thrashes the water with its wings to stir the fish into activity, or flocks of the birds may line up and encircle a school of fish. The pelicans might even drive fish against the shore to more easily capture them with their huge, broad bills. Clever fishermen, the pelicans.

Whether sitting on a wharf piling, swimming in the water, or flying through the air with stately measured wing strokes, the long-billed pelicans are graceful and distinctive birds. They are among the largest of all water birds and are sociable and friendly even when feeding, resting, or nesting. Being nimble fishermen and great fish eaters, they carry their market baskets with them -the capacious, expandable pouch beneath their bills. Pelicans live in warm regions, and although they are aquatic birds—air sacs under their skin make them buoyant—they always stay close to shore.

Above: *Les Pélicans.* 1834. Engraving. From *Le Magasin Pittoresque, Paris.*

Left: *Pelican feeding her young.* Woodcut.

Opposite: *Forêt Tropical.* Detail. 1919. Charles Dufresne. French. Oil on canvas. *Musée Nationale d'Art Moderne, Paris.*

QUAIL

Quails have a long and colorful history, reaching back to early times when the spring quail migration meant feasting for hard-working peasants and herdsmen around the Mediterranean.

Primitive hunters observing the quails' vigorous mating antics considered them a symbol of sex and fertility. In ancient Greece and in the Middle East, the coming of spring was heralded by the quail, for that was the time when enormous flocks flew out of Africa on their way to their breeding grounds in Europe and Asia. According to the Old Testament, quails are the birds that saved the Hebrew people from starvation during their wanderings in the Sinai Desert, after their escape from Egypt. Pet

quails were highly esteemed in ancient Greece and were given as a gift from a young man to his beloved.

Quail fighting, similar to cockfighting, was a popular sport in the Orient. From there it was introduced into Europe. Plutarch, the first-century Greek essayist and biographer, tells us that Julius Caesar was fond of quail fighting and that his birds were often victorious. Shakespeare, drawing on this source, mentions quail fighting in a number of his plays. For a time quail fighting was the vogue in Italy. Two birds were placed at opposite ends of a long table and millet seeds were thrown between them to provoke a quarrel.

In ancient times, the Japanese learned to domesticate quails, breeding them for excellence in song, color, and form. Today, the breeding of quails for their eggs is an important small industry in Japan, producing over 500 million quail eggs a year.

Quails are the smallest members of a family of heavy-bodied land birds and are closely related to partridges, pheasants, and chickens. Native to both the Old and the New Worlds, they have been popular game birds and a favored table delicacy for thousands of years. A distinct group of American quails has evolved in the New World. The most common is the bobwhite, widespread in the eastern part of the United Sates and in the south into Mexico. It is named for its clearly enunciated call, "bobwhite, bob-bobwhite!" Five other species of quail live in the western part of the United States of which the best known is the California quail. Quails are short-tailed, plump birds, nine to eleven inches long, with rounded wings. They nest and forage on the ground, eating seeds, succulent vegetable matter, and some insects.

Quails are friendly, sociable birds. They form large groups, called coveys. With an instinctive sense of self-preservation, the covey forms a circle on the ground at night under dense cover and sleeps with heads pointing outward. In this formation, at least one pair of eyes will be in line with any approaching danger. At the first sign of trouble, the whole flock takes off into the air at once like an exploding bombshell.

Above: *Persian miniature.* Late 18th century. *The Free Library of Philadelphia.*

Opposite: *Iberis umbellata and Tetras Francolinus.* Late 16th–early 17th century. Jacopo Ligozzi. Italian. Engraving. *Gabinetto di Disegni, Uffizi, Florence.*

Left: From *Chinese Cut-Paper Designs.* Selected by Theodore Menten. Dover publications, New York.

STORK

Above: *Scene on the Roofs of Strasbourg.*
Theophile Schuler. Engraving.

Opposite: *Fisherman.* Detail. 1961. Mijo Kovacic.
Yugoslavian. Oil on canvas. *Gallery of Modern
Art, Zagreb, Yugoslavia.*

The stork is probably best known as a symbol of childbirth. Often depicted delivering a newborn baby to a home, the stork is sometimes thought to be the possessor of children's souls. It is also believed the stork finds infants in marshes, ponds, and springs, and that the mere presence of a stork near a home indicates that a birth is imminent.

In many places storks have traditionally been regarded as good-luck symbols, especially white storks. In Germany it is considered auspicious if a stork nests on the roof of a house. At various times in some Mediterranean countries, storks have been protected because of their fondness for eating lizards. To kill a stork would bring bad luck (as well as an enlarged lizard population).

Moroccan belief gave storks less credit. A stork building a nest on a house was believed to presage the home's becoming empty. A nest in a tree would cause the tree to wither. A clean white stork indicated a warm sunny year, while a dirty stork was a sign of a bad year to come.

Other superstitions about storks include the belief that their eggs cure drunkenness; that if storks leave their rooftop nests and build others hurriedly in trees, it is a sign of coming war; that storks leave an area just before a pestilence strikes; and that if storks leave their nests permanently, great calamity for the region is foreseen.

Besides lizards, storks eat small rodents, frogs, water insects, and sometimes carrion. They are waders by nature, inhabiting marshes, river shores, and lakes throughout the tropical and semitropical regions of the world and the warmer parts of the temperate zones.

Medium-large birds, storks have long necks and bills, and long, broad wings but short tails. Storks are strong fliers and soar through the air with their necks extended.

Though the white storks are best known, there are also black-and-white species and some that are black with green, blue, or purple markings.

Perhaps one reason for the association of storks with children is that both the male and female birds are exceptionally good parents to their own offspring. After a nuptial party that includes displays of dancing and posturing, a stork couple builds a platform nest of sticks in a tree or on a ledge of some sort. Three to five eggs are laid, which both parents incubate for about 35 days. The young come into the world naked but soon develop downy coats. They remain in the nest for a relatively long period of time with both parents assiduously attending to their needs.

SWALLOW

Above: From *Chinese Cut-Paper Designs*. Selected by Theodore Menten. Dover Publications, New York.

Opposite: *Garden of Earthly Delights*. Detail, left panel. Late 15th century. Hieronymus Bosch. Dutch. Oil on wood. *Prado, Madrid.*

In ancient Greece, swallows were regarded much as robins are today. Symbols of friendliness, grace, and charm, the arrival of the first swallow in spring was a source of happiness and relief.

Later, Europeans thought of swallows as good-luck charms. One rhyme chanted:

The robin and the wren
Are God's cock and hen,
The swallow and the swift
Are God Almighty's gifts.

Another verse told of the evil to come to one who harmed a swallow:

And if in any's hand she chance to die
'Tis counted ominous, I know not why.

Certain characteristics of the swallow gave rise to the belief that because of its rapid twittering it might be a cure for diseases involving frenzy, such as epilepsy. The red breasts of some species caused the swallow to be honored as the bringer of fire from heaven to earth. Seasonal migrations linked swallows to the rites of spring and fertility.

Swallows are small, sparrow-sized, graceful birds. They have wide mouths that can catch many insects even while the birds swoop to and fro. Because they eat mosquitoes, swallows are often welcomed especially in damp areas. The largest swallow found in the United States, commonly called the purple martin, has quite a reputation for its mosquito-eating abilities.

A pleasant relationship exists between the farmer and the barn swallow. The farmer provides excellent places for the barn swallow to build its mud nest. In return, the barn swallow helps to limit the population of insects that accompany farm animals. In addition to nesting in barns, other swallows nest in trees, along the banks of streams, on cliffs, and often, to mankind's delight, in birdhouses.

The tails of most swallows are deeply forked. There are several stories that seek to explain the cause of this characteristic. In one story it is said the swallow's tail feathers were burned by the Devil when the bird brought fire down from heaven to benefit man. Another tale says the feathers were snatched out by the Devil's fire guard, the sparrow. Yet another says the forked tail is the result of an injury by a sky god named Tengri, who shot the bird with an arrow. Whatever the cause, the swallow's forked tail aids it in flight. And it is the distinctive swooping flight that makes the swallow such a graceful addition to the world of birds.

SWAN

The swan holds a prominent place in history. Even Stone Age rock carvings picture swans and there are numerous folktales that involve or center on the swan. Most likely it is the swan's commanding appearance that has attracted so much attention. The largest of waterfowl, swans are closely related to geese and ducks but are more dramatic looking. Their gracefully curved necks are often longer than their large bodies. Most species are pure white except for black or orange markings on bills or necks. However, there is a black swan with white wing tips that is native to and a national symbol of Australia.

Swans are good fliers, traveling in V-formation groups with each swan's neck extended. Their webbed feet make them good swimmers, but adult swans cannot dive. Instead, as they reach for aquatic plants, they must extend their long necks and sensitive bills.

Although swans are most often seen in pairs, it is difficult to tell the sexes apart. Swans live to a great age, some up to 80 years, and often as lifelong mates. Though there are stable populations of most kinds of swans, the largest North American

species, the trumpeter swan, almost became extinct until preservation efforts brought the species' population back into the thousands.

The most widespread folktale concerning swans is the legend of the swan maiden. Told in various forms in Asia, Europe, Australia, Polynesia, North and South America, and parts of Africa, the legend probably had its origin in early Sanskrit writings. The tale is of a beautiful maiden who could transform herself into either human or swan form, with the aid of a magic object—a feather robe, ring, or chain. A young man found the magic object, hid it while the maiden was human, and then married her. Alas, she eventually found the object and returned to the swan form.

One of the happier stories about swans is Hans Christian Andersen's tale, *The Ugly Duckling*. In this story a swan baby is orphaned and adopted by a duck family. As an infant, the swan is uglier than the ducklings and is ostracized by them. As the swan and ducklings mature, however, the swan turns into a beautiful creature while the ducks remain rather plain. This story has brought hope and comfort to many children who consider themselves odd or uglier than their peers.

The ancient Greeks associated swans with many of their gods. They believed that swans were voiceless until just before death, when they uttered one beautiful song. Though this has been proven untrue, the phrase swan song is today used to describe a final creative act before death.

Above: *Magazine illustration*. February, 1897. Max Wislicenus. German. *Jugend, Munich*.

Left: *Family crest*. From *Fairbairn's Book of Crests of the Families of Great Britain and Ireland*. Jack Fairbairn. Jack, London.

Opposite: *Swans on a Lake*. Art Nouveau Poster.

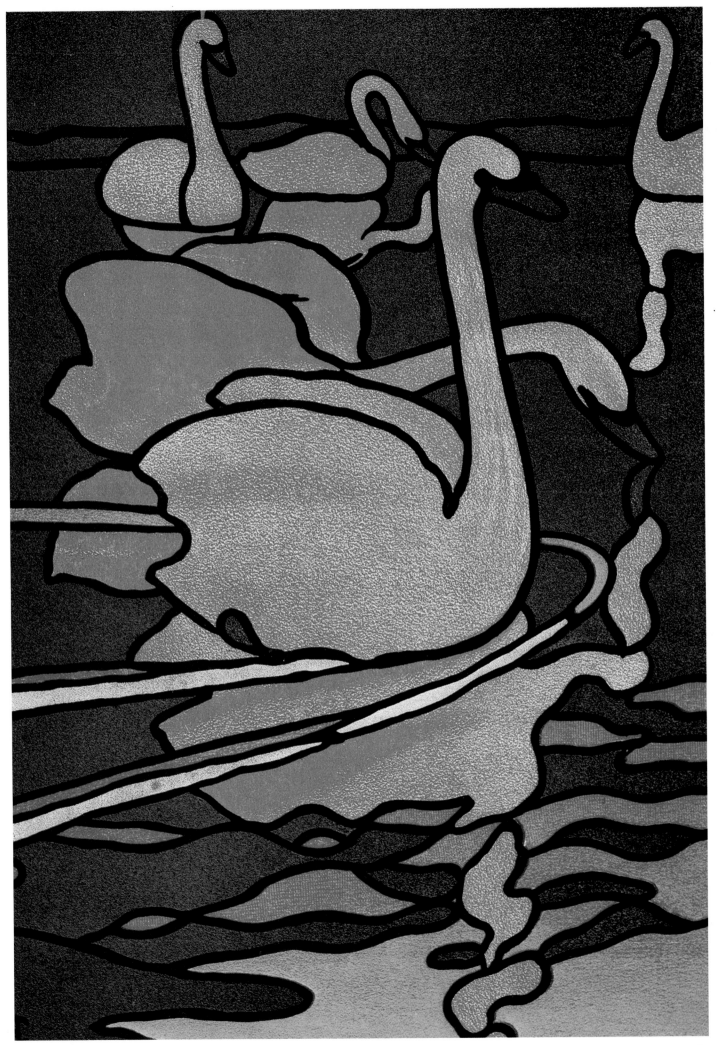

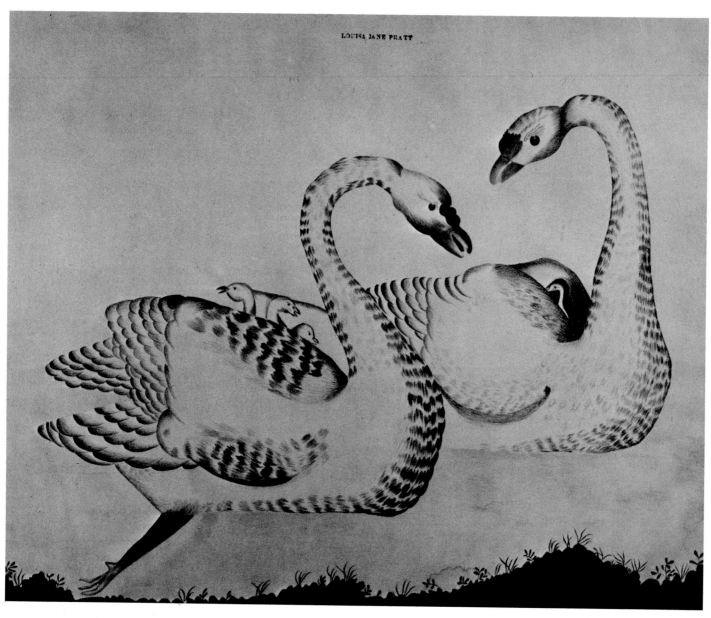

Above: *Two Swans.* 19th century. Louisa Jane Pratt. American. Watercolor. *Collection of Barbara Johnson, New Jersey.*

Opposite: *Leda and the Swan.* 16th century. Leonardo da Vinci. Italian. Oil on canvas. *Galleria Borghese, Rome.*

THRUSH

Above: *Group of thrushes*. Engraving. From *The New Natural History*. Richard Lydekker. Merrill and Baker, New York.

Opposite: *Still Life with Eggs*. Detail. 70 A.D. Pompeiian. Fresco.

Some of the poetry of everyday life is given form and expression in the lovely songs of birds whose music can transform a secluded shady dell into a sylvan concert hall. And there is no family of birds that can better perform this ear-soothing magic than the brown-backed, spot-breasted song thrush. The torrent of melodic sound that pours from these modestly colored birds affirms the observation that birds lacking in visual splendor are among the most gifted of all singers. Whereas the brightly plumaged birds advertise themselves by bringing color and drama to a landscape, the drab birds whose colorings melt into their surroundings can flutter into the sky and fill it and the land below with rhapsodic sound.

The thrush family is to be found in both the Old and the New Worlds. They are small to medium-sized birds. Their legs are rather long for songbirds; they have large eyes and moderately slender bills, suitable for scratching for their favorite earthworms or insects or feeding on ripened berries. They fly and perch freely but feed mostly on the ground. They will take a few hops, pause for a moment, then pick up a worm or toss aside a leaf to better scan the ground for a tasty morsel. Trim, quiet, deliberate, the thrush lives in woodlands or semiwooded areas.

Among the best known of the thrushes are the hermit thrush, the wood thrush, the olive-backed thrush (also known as Swainson's thrush), the gray-cheeked thrush, and the veery. It takes a keen eye to identify each because in many cases the differences are subtle. The silvery rich, bell-like tones of the hermit thrush are considered the most beautiful of any American bird, comparable only to the voice of the European nightingale. Some of the thrushes are extremely shy and elusive, singing only from unapproachable tangles of forests and woods. The birds sing most eloquently just before dusk.

It is not surprising that the lilting rhythms and rippling melodies of these songbirds have inspired poets since earliest times. Shakespeare, Tennyson, and Hardy, among others, have singled out the thrush for special mention. Robert Browning called particular attention to the thrush's pattern of repeating its musical phrasing:

*That's the wise thrush; he sings each
song twice over,
Lest you should think he never could
recapture
The first fine careless rapture!*

TURKEY

THE·INLAND·PRINTER
THANKSGIVING·NUMBER·VOL·XIV·NO·2·1894

NOVEMBER, 1894.

The Burr McIntosh Monthly.

Brillat-Savarin, the distinguished French gastronome, paid the turkey the supreme compliment when he wrote "It is surely one of the prettiest presents the Old World has received from the New." Turkeys were unknown in Europe until the Spanish conquistadors brought a few birds back to Spain from Mexico around 1520. The meaty, tasty birds with their succulent white breasts found a welcome place on European dining tables, supplanting the peacock, which had been the favored delicacy. Within a couple of decades, the English were serving turkey for Christmas dinner. When the Pilgrims and other early settlers arrived in New England, they were overjoyed to find wild turkeys similar to the tame ones they had left behind.

It is curious that turkey, a name that suggests the Near East, should be applied to a fowl that is completely American and exclusively New World in its association. There are many theories but little agreement about the etymology of the name. The French called the bird *poule d'indie,* "chicken of India," because America was thought of as part of the West Indies. Later this was shortened to *dindon* for a male or tom turkey, *dinde* for the hen. In Spain, where the turkey is considered a kind of peacock, it is called *pavo,* an old name for peacock. The Portuguese named it *peru,* for they knew it came from Spain's American colonies and at that time the Portuguese referred to all Spanish America as Peru.

The American Indians valued the turkey greatly not only for food but also for the feathers, which they used for decorations, and the bones, out of which they made whistles. The bird was a heroic figure in their myths. It helped in the creation of the world and was the foe of evil spirits. Not only did the turkey show the people how to raise corn and other crops, but according to one legend, also taught the Indians to use tobacco and to roll cigarettes. Some tribes believed that it had a sinister aspect instead; sorcerers would turn themselves into wild turkeys and stalk the Indian villages at night, causing trouble.

The common wild turkey is the ancestor of all domestic breeds. They were fearless, inquisitive birds, and the New World abounded in them. As populations increased and forest lands were cleared, the wild turkeys disappeared, for they need woods to live in. With conservation methods now in force, their numbers are slowly increasing. In addition, domesticated turkeys are bred on turkey farms, and many millions of birds are raised each year—many more than ever roamed the primeval forests in pre-Columbian days.

Benjamin Franklin was eager for the turkey to become the national bird of the United States in preference to the bald eagle. Of the avian controversy, he said, "…the Turkey is a much more respectable Bird, and withal a true native of America."

Opposite left: Cover for *The Inland Printer.*
November, 1894. William H. Bradley. Ameri-
can. Pen and ink. *The Metropolitan Museum of Art,
New York.* Gift of Fern Bradley Dufner, 1952.

Opposite right: *The Burr McIntosh—Monthly.*
November, 1903. C. Hobart. Color lithograph.

Above: *The Turkeys.* 1877. Claude Monet.
French. Oil on canvas. *Jeu de Paume, Paris.*

VULTURE

A vulture soaring effortlessly through a bright clear sky or perched on a tree with wings outspread is a majestic sight, although the bird is far less attractive on closer inspection. Its harshly contoured head and neck, naked and unfeathered, and habit of feeding on carrion have combined to make it unloved and unadmired.

As far back as Roman times, vulture was an opprobrious term applied to greedy or hardhearted people. The feeling of sanctity, respect, or even awe with which many ancients viewed birds of great size was rarely extended to the vulture. John Milton, the seventeenth-century English poet, using birds in his poetry to symbolize human vices, characterized Satan as a vulture.

The name vulture is applied to a group of birds that share the common trait of feeding on carrion. Unlike their distant relatives–hawks and eagles which hunt their own food–vultures specialize in scavenging. The North American vultures are quite distinct from those in the Old World, but both follow the same lifestyle. Among the American vultures are the turkey vulture with its small-beaked red head, which somewhat resembles the turkey; the smaller black vulture or carrion crow; and the tropical king vulture with its cream and black plumage and gaily colored head. They are voiceless, emitting weak hisses.

Vultures have weak beaks and claws, a characteristic of carrion eaters. Since they do not grapple with live prey, they have no need for a powerful bite or grip. Some

Left: *Soaring.* 1951. Andrew Wyeth. American. Tempera on masonite. *Shelburne Museum, Shelburne, Vermont.*

Below: *Group of turkey vultures.* Engraving. From *The New Natural History.* Richard Lydekker. Merrill and Baker, New York.

species do occasionally hunt, but they will attack only helpless little animals such as young birds or baby mammals.

Many vultures have extremely keen vision and find their food by sight rather than by scent. A vulture will circle in the air for hours, tirelessly and patiently, and swoop down when it spies an animal that is dead or dying. Apparently vultures watch each other as attentively as they watch the ground because within a few hours scores or even hundreds will converge for the feast. Vultures are normally solitary birds, but they will gather in crowds to feed, standing around in a ring at a safe distance until they are certain that the animal is dead. The larger and more aggressive vultures may frighten the weaker ones away with menacing hisses and gestures.

The vulture is a greedy and voracious eater, and it is not unusual for a bird that has gorged itself to be unable to fly when it has finished eating. However, the greed can be an aid to survival for there can be a long interval between meals.

But in spite of the unpleasantness associated with vultures, they perform a valuable public service as self-appointed members of a cleaning brigade, devouring dead animals that might otherwise pollute the environment. The food belt provided by animals killed by speeding cars on highways is an endless one needing constant vigilance. For their contribution toward maintaining a healthier environment, vultures are often protected by law.

WREN

The drab plumage of the little brown wren in no way matches the joyous melody that bubbles from its tiny throat. Perched on a bush with its tail feathers cocked high in the air, the wren warbles and trills, delivering a stream of musical sounds that are incredibly large for the small body that produces them.

Interest in the wren has been traced back to an ancient pagan religion where the wren was sacred to the earth gods. The wren was also believed to have brought the gift of fire to humans, scorching its feathers in the process; hence its black-streaked brown plumage. In some parts of Europe the wren was thought to be in league with the Devil, and in other parts a contradictory belief that the wren was a pet of the Virgin Mary prevailed. In the United States the back-country people of the Ozark Mountains once believed that the bite of a wren was poisonous because the bird ate so many spiders. But in spite of the legend and folklore, this beguiling bird with its cheery song is a universal favorite.

A tale is told of all the birds gathering to choose a king. After a heated discussion that threatened to erupt into violence, the birds decided that the one who flew the highest would be king. Up they fluttered and one by one returned, unable to compete with the eagle soaring high above them. Just as the eagle was about to proclaim its victory, the air was filled with melodious warbling from a wren flying overhead. The little creature had perched on the eagle's back at the start of the contest and, still fresh and rested, had no difficulty flapping a bit higher to win the coveted award.

Wrens are primarily an American family, but they are also found in Europe and Asia. Certain characteristics are shared by nearly all of the various species of the wren family. They are bundles of nervous energy, always hopping and flitting about. They can be bold to the point of impudence as they pop in and out of tangles of shrubbery or jumbles of rock, scolding a stray cat or bossily driving another bird off their territory. This trait was recognized by an anonymous poet in the tenth century who wrote in one of his poems "A nimble singer, the combative brown wren..."

Left: *Book illustration*. Late 19th century. From *Tierleben im Ornament*. G. Sturm. Hoffman, Stuttgart, Germany.

Opposite: *La Cage*. Detail. 18th century. François Boucher, French.